SUMMARY

of

LIFESPAN

by David Sinclair

Why We Age and Why We Don't Have to

Spark Reads

Note to readers:

This is an unofficial summary & analysis of **David Sinclair**'s *"Lifespan"* designed to enrich your reading experience. Buy the original book here.

approved, licensed, or endorsed by the aforementioned interests or any of their licensees.

The information in this book has been provided for educational and entertainment purposes only.

The information contained in this book has been compiled from sources deemed reliable and it is accurate to the best of the Author's knowledge; however, the Author cannot guarantee its accuracy and validity and cannot be held liable for any errors or omissions. Upon using the information contained in this book, you agree to hold harmless the author from and against any damages, costs, and expenses, including any legal fees, potentially resulting from the application of any of the information provided by this guide. The disclaimer applies to any damages or injury caused by the use and application, whether directly or indirectly, of any advice or information presented, whether for breach of contract, tort, neglect, personal injury, criminal intent, or under any other cause of action. You agree to accept all risks of using the information presented inside this book.

The fact that an individual or organization is referred to in this document as a citation or source of

My Free Gift to You

As A Way to Say "Thank You" For Being a Fan of Our Series, I've included a Free Gift for You: A report on How to Lead in All Aspects of Your Life. For You, Free.

If you'd like one, please visit:

https://sparkreads.clickfunnels.com/pg-freegift

The Spark Reads Team

Table Contents

Summary of Lifespan: Why We Age and Why We Don't Have to

*L*ifespan by David Sinclair is an incredible and educating journey into the world of aging research and medical advancement. Sinclair proposes and meticulously lays out a rather radical picture of aging. His strong and confident views in the book are rooted in his belief that aging is a disease — one that can be cured. He details the cutting-edge science being carried out in the field of longevity and how scientists are gradually shifting away from erroneous assumptions about aging.

Assisted by contributing writer Matthew LaPlante, Sinclair asserts that the phenomenon of aging, which we have relentlessly embraced as being inevitable, actually results from DNA damage that is both identifiable and curable. He offers somewhat radical and disruptive narratives on aging — often closely followed by scientific evidence. While he doesn't offer a definitive cure to aging, Sinclair outlines several pharmaceuticals currently in development as well as ongoing research that could potentially counteract aging. He also harmonizes medical research, historical analysis, and personal experiences in an attempt to transmogrify our views on aging. This thrilling yet provocative work takes readers to the forefront of the medical research that is pushing our perceived scientific limitations regarding the primordial concept of aging. In doing so, Sinclair reveals incredible breakthroughs in the field — some from his own research — which demonstrate how we can slow down, or even possibly reverse, aging. The key to achieving this, he explains, is by activating newly-discovered genes that have evolved from an ancient genetic survival circuit that is both the cause of aging and the key to reversing it. He outlines dozens of scientific research studies that reinforce the promise that in the near future, we will enjoy incredibly longer and healthier lives.

David Sinclair maybe a lifelong medical geneticist, but his book isn't just concerned with relaying his lab-tested research on longevity. He takes a somewhat antagonistic view of his research by weighing the implication of greatly prolonging human lives, discussing the potential effects this could have on politics, availability of resources, climate change, and a host of other possible consequences. However, just as with the optimism he expresses over several noble ideas throughout the book, Sinclair believes the human race's ingenuity will find a fix for whatever consequences prolonged human existence may possibly bring. He asserts that there is no biological law that says we must age; as such, it is unreasonable to settle for its inevitability. While Sinclair makes truly eyebrow-raising statements in the book at times, he does not at any point promise immortality. Nonetheless, he does promise a not-so-distant future in which medicine will help us live much healthier and longer lives — at least, if the scientific variables he wagers on come through as expected.

Part 1: What We Know (The Past)

Chapter One: Viva Primordium

In Chapter One, Sinclair begins with a description of an uninhabitable planet — essentially, the planet Earth as it likely was billions of years ago. He paints a picture of this planet as being a hot, volcanic, tumultuous, and ruthlessly unforgiving place. Its atmosphere was unlike that of the Earth today — it was a humid, toxic blanket of nitrogen, methane, and carbon dioxide. Even as this planet was inhabitable, Sinclair describes a series of gradual changes in its chemistry that made room for the birth of the world's first RNA molecules, the predecessors to DNA. This signaled the beginning of life on this planet. Sinclair also describes a series of biological evolutions that lead to the birth of complex life forms. He discusses a life form he calls the Magna superstes (meaning the great survivor) – the only one among several early species that was able to evolve thanks to a genetic survival mechanism. Within the allegedly brutal planet it found itself, the Magna superstes was armed with the ability to hunker down when the going got tough, diverting most of its energy into activities that ensured its survival. This enabled the Magna superstes to survive different and often complicated evolutionary steps to become the origin of archaea, bacteria, fungi, plants, and animals.

Today, after a long line of evolutionary steps, Sinclair points out that we still have this ancient primordial survival kit in all of us. From plants and animals to fungus, this survival kit is present in every living thing that shares the planet with us. An advanced version of this survival mechanism, present in humans, is what allows us to survive for decades. However, the mutations that this survival mechanism has gone through over its previous numerous evolutionary steps are the reason we age — the singular reason! After establishing this important premise, Sinclair goes on to discuss aging specifically. He explains that many biologists and gerontologists (doctors who specialize in aging) often don't investigate the root cause of aging, but are usually more concerned with treating the consequences that come with it. He explains that the somewhat myopic approach to aging we see today is akin to the approach toward cancer in the 1960s. During this period, the fight against cancer revolved around quenching or ameliorating its consequences. It was essentially a fight against its symptoms rather than the problem itself. A favorable paradigm shift within cancer research and the fight against it only gained traction in the 1970s, when microbiologists discovered the genes that cause cancer when they undergo mutation. Sinclair is of the opinion that research on aging today is at a similar level as cancer research was in the 1960s. Just as we left cancer to fate in the 1960s, we have unfortunately submitted ourselves to the inevitability of aging.

Before Wilbur and Orville Wright built a flying machine — something that was thought impossible — they needed knowledge of airflow, negative pressure, and wind tunnels. Before the United States could put men on the moon, they needed an understanding of metallurgy, liquid combustion, and computers. Similarly, David Sinclair opines that if we are to make real progress in tackling aging and its consequences, we must first arrive at a unified explanation for why we age, not simply at the evolutionary level but also the fundamental level. However, he explains that the different attempts to come to an all-fitting explanation for aging have been without much luck. Historically, some scientists theorized aging as being caused by free radicals and DNA mutation. Among some such theories was the "Free Radical Theory of Aging," posited by Denham Harman, then a chemist for shell oil. Harman blamed aging on unpaired electrons that whizzed around within cells, damaging DNA through oxidation. Harman, along with hundreds of other researchers, tested this theory, but the result did not indicate any scientific breakthroughs; Harman's theory blaming free radicals as the universal cause of aging has since been disproved and disregarded, because the damage free radicals cause don't actually lead to aging.

Similarly, two other scientists, Peter Medawar and Leo Szilard, were at the forefront of research linking aging to mutation. Both argued that aging was caused by DNA damage and the resulting loss of genetic information. Other scientists also postulated similar hypotheses that pointed to mutation as the cause of aging. The idea that accumulated mutation was the cause of aging was embraced by the public and scientific community alike during the 1950s and the 1960s. However, it didn't take long before this new

7

narrative was disproved by several pieces of research. Studies on cloning and the fact that this is even possible gave the answer as to whether or not mutations cause aging. If old cells indeed lost crucial genetic information (as argued by Medawar and Szilard) and this was the cause of aging, we shouldn't be able to clone new animals from older individuals, since the cells must have lost the genetic information required to do so successfully. If possible at all, clones would be born old.

As different theories about the cause of aging continued to emerge, new discoveries and research continued to disprove their validity. However, eventually, the ideas of leading scientists in the field began to coalesce around a new model. This new model had an answer for why the brilliant scientists of the past couldn't find a single cause of aging. It was because there wasn't one sole cause. Instead, the new model describes aging and its consequences as being the result of several "hallmarks" of aging, namely:

- Genomic instability caused by DNA damage
- Attrition of the protective chromosomal endcaps, the telomeres

- Alterations to the epigenome that controls which genes are turned on and off
- Loss of healthy protein maintenance, known as proteostasis
- Deregulated nutrient sensing caused by metabolic changes
- Mitochondrial dysfunction
- Accumulation of senescent zombie-like cells that inflame healthy cells
- Exhaustion of stem cells
- Altered intercellular communication and the production of inflammatory molecules

Scientists have settled on these hallmarks of aging. The consensus is that if you address any one of them, you can slow down aging. Alternatively, if you can address all of them, you may not age at all. Taking into consideration all of these hallmarks, Sinclair proposes a single cause of aging — the loss of information. However, Sinclair's idea of "loss of information" being the cause of aging is different from that theorized by Szilard and Medawar. Unlike the duo's theory, which focused on the loss of robust digital information in the form of DNA,

Sinclair opines that aging is caused by the loss of analog information.

The survival circuit that was present in the Magna superstes has evolved over the years, and today, scientists have found over two dozen of them within the human genome. These survival circuits or longevity genes have been shown to possess the ability to extend both the average and maximum lifespans in many organisms. They don't just make life longer; they also make it healthier, which is why they can also be thought of as "vitality genes." Since their discovery, scientists have focused a lot of attention on them. These genes have been proven to be manipulable in ways that can offer longer and healthier lives. Some of these genes include the sirtuins, NAD, and target of rapamycin (TOR) and the AMPK.

Sirtuins: These are at the forefront of medical research and drug development due to their enormous potential. In short, sirtuins are what order our bodies to hunker down in times of stress and protect us against the major diseases of aging like diabetes, heart disease, Alzheimer's disease, cancer, and osteoporosis. They are also responsible for muting the chronic, overactive inflammation that drives diseases such as metabolic disorders, atherosclerosis, ulcerative colitis, arthritis, and asthma. They prevent cell death and boost mitochondria, the power packs of the cell. Their powers are enormous, and science has established most of them in peer-reviewed studies.

TOR: Target of rapamycin or TOR is another set of genes that performs functions similar to sirtuins. TOR is made up of complex proteins that regulate growth and metabolism. Just like sirtuins, researchers have found TOR – called mTOR in mammals – in every organism they've examined. mTOR can also signal cells in stress to hunker down and improve survival by boosting such activities as DNA repair and reducing inflammation.

AMPK: This is a metabolic control enzyme that has evolved to respond to low energy levels, activating glucose and fatty acid uptake and oxidation when cellular energy is low. Just like sirtuins and TOR, science has learned a lot about it.

NAD: Nicotinamide adenine dinucleotide (NAD) is a critical coenzyme found in every cell in the body. NAD helps turn nutrients into energy, working like a personal assistant for proteins that regulate other cellular functions such as sirtuins. It's involved in hundreds of metabolic processes, but our levels of NAD decline with age. The loss of NAD as we age and the resulting decline in sirtuin activity is thought to be a primary reason why bodies start developing diseases when we are old but not when we are young.

Chapter Two: The Demented Pianist

In Chapter Two, David Sinclair narrates his long journey toward formulating the information behind the theory of aging. Describing several research studies on the topic, both by him and other scientists, he lays out how the loss of analog information has influenced aging. Before arriving at his theory of aging, Sinclair started out his research with yeast. While humans are separated from yeast by over a billion years of evolution, he believed we still have a lot in common, and that there was a lot to learn about humans from yeast. Sinclair set out to understand aging by first studying the Werner Syndrome – a rare disease that mimics the consequences of old age with symptoms like loss of body strength, wrinkles, gray hair, hair loss, cataracts, osteoporosis, heart problems, and many other telltale signs. Not long into his research efforts, another scientist, George Martin, announced the discovery of the gene that, when mutated, caused Werner syndrome. After the discovery of the Werner gene, known as the WRN, Sinclair set out to test if a similar gene – known as Slow Growth Suppressor 1, or SGS1 in yeast – when mutated, would cause Werner syndrome in yeast. His test was affirmative. After swapping healthy SGS1 with its mutated version, the yeast exhibited signs of aging. After achieving these results, Sinclair became convinced that he could use yeast to more rapidly determine the cause of Werner syndrome and better understand aging in general.

In the course of his research with yeast, Sinclair was able to make better sense of aging, unraveling two more important concepts in the process – epigenetic noise and loss of cell identity. The analog information, whose loss Sinclair had blamed for aging, resides in what is known as the epigenome, and because it is analog, it is prone to epigenetic "noise." This noise, which is basically inconsistencies or changes in our genes and enzymes, can trigger the hallmarks of aging. Sinclair was also able to establish that the fundamental and upstream cause of sterility and aging in yeast was the inherent instability of the genome. He went even further; through his research on yeast, and subsequently, mammalian cells, he was able to reconcile the disparate factors of aging into one universal model. His model illustrated that broken DNA causes genome instability, which in turn causes disruption of DNA packaging and gene regulation (the epigenome), leading to loss of cell identity, cellular senescence, and subsequent disease and death in that order. The implication of his model was profound; if an intervention could be made at any of the steps, people might be able to live longer.

Using the knowledge from their research on yeast, David Sinclair and his lab colleagues focused on identifying the mechanism for aging in humans. The result of their studies asserted that the malfunction of a family of proteins called sirtuins is the single cause of aging. Sirtuins are responsible for repairing DNA damage and overall cellular health by keeping cells on task. In other words, they are what tell kidney cells to act like kidney cells, liver cells to act like liver cells, and skin cells to act like skin cells. When the sirtuins become overwhelmed, cells lose their identity, fail to execute their responsibilities, and start to misbehave, which is when the symptoms of aging such as wrinkles or organ failure set in. The genetic information in our cells remains intact even when we get older, but our bodies eventually lose the ability to interpret it. This is due to the fact that our bodies start to run low on NAD – a molecule that activates sirtuins – as we age. Without NAD, sirtuins can't do their job, and without this, the cells in our bodies forget what they're supposed to be doing – thus the hallmarks of aging kick in.

Chapter Three: The Blind Epidemic

In Chapter Three, David Sinclair begins by describing an event that was hosted by the Royal Society of London for Improving Natural Knowledge. In attendance were several luminaries from diverse fields of scientific research. Over the course of the event, nineteen different scientists from some of the best research institutions in the world presented their findings on topics related to aging. In the end, they all came to a rather provocative conclusion – that aging is not an inevitable part of life, but rather a "disease process with a broad spectrum of pathological consequences." Sinclair's view on aging is strongly aligned with this consensus. In Chapter Three, he criticizes the world's acceptance of aging as being an inevitable natural occurrence. He emphasizes that aging is a disease – one that can be treated. He points out that aging "fulfills every category of what we call a disease except one: it impacts more than half the population." Unfortunately, because this fails to satisfy this component of the medical community's definition of a disease, aging doesn't "fit nicely into the system we've built for funding medical research, drug development, and the reimbursement of medical costs by insurance companies." The implication of this is that aging doesn't get the attention it deserves, but only the consequences that come with it. While aging itself is a disease and an "ultimate risk factor," we are pursuing cures for individual diseases like cancer, heart disease, and Alzheimer's, most of which are triggered by the aging process.

When people die, doctors and public health officials record both the immediate and underlying causes of disability and death. This information is used by both medical leaders and policymakers around the world to make public health decisions. Generally speaking, the more a particular cause of death shows up, the more society and policymakers are likely to show concern toward fighting it. This is why ailments like heart disease, diabetes, and dementia are currently major focuses of research and interventional medical care, while aging is not. Even though aging is the greatest cause of all these diseases, aging itself is, in David Sinclair's view, disregarded by most as natural and inevitable. He emphasizes that this attitude toward aging is flawed. As he puts it: "There is nothing more dangerous to us than age. Yet we have conceded its power over us. And we have turned our fight for better health in other directions."

According to him, one of the best ways to predict whether someone will survive a medical condition is how old he or she is when diagnosed. The same ailments that a teenager may escape from unscathed may prove life-altering or even fatal for someone much older. A hip fracture, for instance, is something a teenager should be expected to bounce back from. However, for someone older, perhaps 50, such an injury could be a life-altering event. For someone even older, maybe 65, that same injury could be fatal. According to Sinclair, some reports indicate that half of the people who are over the age of 65 who suffer a hip fracture will likely die within six months. Similarly, wounds heal much more slowly for aged individuals and could potentially be very dangerous. An unsuspecting foot injury that should easily heal for a younger person could be deadly for aged persons. The older we get, the higher the probability that an injury or illness will drive us to our death. It might be a particular disease that actually pulls the trigger, but it's the "aging disease" that put the gun in its hand. In

Sinclair's own words: "Separating aging from disease obfuscates a truth about how we reach the ends of our lives: though it's certainly important to know why someone fell from a cliff, it's equally important to know what brought that person to the precipice in the first place."

Sinclair uses these points to build his argument that aging should be seen through a different lens. He argues that if it were diseases like hepatitis, kidney disease, or melanoma that brought us the sort of susceptibility that aging does, we would put those diseases on a list of the deadliest illnesses in the world. He adds that when we discovered that smoking accelerates the aging clock and makes us more likely to die younger, we fought it. Indeed, we are still fighting it with public health campaigns, class action lawsuits, taxes on tobacco products, and legislation. When we knew that cancer makes us more likely to die, we also fought it with billions of dollars' worth of research aimed at putting an end to it. However, though we've known for some time that aging makes you more likely to die, unlike other diseases, we've accepted it as part of life. He likens this thinking to accepting that diseases like diabetes or cancer are irreversible or inevitable. While our modern medical systems are built to address these individual diseases to stop us from dying – at least before our time – they fail to realize that stopping "the progression of one disease doesn't make it any less likely that a person will die of another." He explains: "Surviving cancer or heart disease doesn't substantially increase the average human lifespan; it just decreases the odds of dying of cancer or heart disease."

Sinclair further reemphasizes the notion of aging being the ultimate risk factor. He explains that while smoking increases an individual's risk of getting cancer by fivefold, being 50 years old increases that risk to a hundredfold, and being 70, a thousand fold. He bemoans that such an exponential increase is not reason enough to allocate more resources toward the treatment of aging. He questions why society chooses to focus solely on individual ailments if we could address the root cause of a problem that impacts us all – especially if, in doing so, we could significantly impact all those other individual diseases.

Part 2: What We're Learning (The Present)

Chapter Four: Longevity Now

In Chapter Four, David Sinclair discusses the application of the wealth of knowledge on aging outlined in earlier chapters and shares practical steps we can take to enhance longevity and vitality. Through research-backed methods, he identifies and explains ways our primordial survival circuit can be activated. He outlines calorie restriction, amino acid restriction, exercise, and exposure to less-than-comfortable temperatures as effective tools we can use to engage or activate our survival circuit. The commonality of our longevity genes or our entire primordial survival network is that they are activated by some level of biological stress. Sinclair illustrates that the aforementioned techniques can provide the right level of biological stress needed to trigger and effectively engage our survival circuit.

Caloric restriction: Sinclair explains that when we eat less, usually large enough to avoid malnutrition but small enough to cause biological stress, we can effectively extend our lifespan and enjoy better health. In his words: "One surefire way to stay healthy longer, one thing you can do to maximize your lifespan right now, it's this: eat less." As counterintuitive as it may sound, Sinclair emphasizes that depriving ourselves of the generally recommended number of calories for some time is unquestionably good for our health and longevity. He points out that this isn't an entirely new or revolutionary science; as far back as the fifteen century, some people were aware of this and actively practiced it. Though history indicates these people who practiced some form of caloric restriction lived longer, scientific attestation to the claim came only after research on caloric restriction on rats was carried out during the First World War. The researchers, Lafayette Mendel, Thomas Osborne, and Edna Ferry, discovered that female rats whose growth was stunted due to lack of food early in life lived much longer than those that had enough to eat. Picking up on that evidence, a similar study on rats in 1935 yielded similar results. In this study, Clive McCay, a researcher from Cornell University, demonstrated that rats fed a diet containing 20 percent indigestible cellulose lived significantly longer lives than those that were fed a typical lab diet. Another study on calorie restriction was done on yeast with similar results; yeast cells fed with lower doses of glucose lived longer than those fed with more. Ever since these first studies were conducted decades ago, research has demonstrated time and again that calorie restriction without malnutrition leads to longevity for all sorts of life forms.

According to Sinclair, there are many practical and sustainable ways to practice calorie restriction, including intermittent fasting, the 16:8 diets, and the 5:2 diets. Intermittent fasting involves eating normal portions of food but with periodic episodes without meals. The 16:8 diets involves skipping breakfast and having a late launch, while the 5:2 diet involves taking 75 percent fewer calories for two days a week.

Amino acid restriction: Amino acids are vital for our survival. They are the organic compounds that serve as the building blocks for every protein in the human body – we'd die quite quickly without them. Nonetheless, even as we can't live without amino acids, research shows we can do ourselves a favor by limiting the amount we put into our bodies. Just like calorie restriction, limiting our intake of amino acids can engage our primordial survival circuit in a way that improves vitality and longevity. Sinclair cites a study by Harvard Medical School that supports this claim. In the study, mice were fed a diet with low levels of amino acid methionine over several years. The results showed that low levels of amino acid methionine worked particularly well to switch on the mice's bodily defenses, protect their organs from hypoxia during surgery, and most importantly, increase their healthy lifespan by 20 percent. In as much as totally depriving ourselves of amino acid would be disastrous, eating only meat – a rich source of all nine essential amino acids – isn't a path to a longer life either. Sinclair explains that we can get just enough of it to keep going from plant-only sources. Plants contain just enough amino acids to keep our engines running, but few enough to induce biological stress that triggers the survival circuit to hunker down, improving overall health and longevity (as ironic as it may sound).

Exercise: This has always been the go-to tool for improved vitality for centuries. However, there was little proof as to exactly how it improved vitality and longevity. Apart from mere anecdotal evidence, Sinclair explains the science behind exercise as a longevity and vitality tool. As we know, the shortening of the telomere has long been known as a hallmark of aging. Sinclair explains that exercising delays the erosion or shortening of the telomere. According to him, when researchers studied the telomeres in the blood cells of thousands of adults with all sorts of diverse exercise habits, they noticed an important correlation: those who exercised more had longer telomeres. A similar study funded by the Centers for Disease Control and Prevention showed that individuals who exercise more – the equivalent of at least 30 minutes of jogging five days a week – have telomeres that appear to be nearly a decade younger than those who live a more sedentary life. This is possible because exercise exerts biological stress on our bodies in a way that activates our survival circuit. Our survival circuit, in turn, packages our telomeres in a way that ensures they are protected against degradation, effectively enhancing longevity and vitality.

Less-than-comfortable temperatures: Building on the foundation of biological stress activating our survival circuit, Sinclair explains that exposing our bodies to less-than-comfortable temperatures can induce biological stress and is a very effective way of turning on our longevity genes. He cites a research study by the Scripps Research Institute I which genetically engineered mice were made to live their lives half degree cooler than normal. The results, he explains, supports his claim: the mice experienced a 20 percent longer life (for female mice), the equivalent of about seven additional healthy human years, while male mice got an extension of 12 percent. Sinclair also explains similar research in yeasts, this time using higher temperatures. According to him, when yeast temperature is increased from 30°C to 37°C, just below the limits of what it can sustain, it lived 30 percent longer. However, he also explains that while colder temperatures have proven beneficial to humans, research on hotter temperatures on humans is mostly inconclusive. Nonetheless, there are several convincing pieces of evidence to support the claim. In a study, over 2,300 middle-aged men from Finland were tracked for more than twenty years. Of all of them, those who used a sauna with greater frequency (up to seven times a week) experienced a twofold drop in heart disease, fatal heart attacks, and all-cause mortality events than those who used the sauna just once a week. Sinclair also discusses some other experiences, some merely anecdotal, that may support the idea that controlled exposure to high temperatures may be able to help us slow down the aging process.

Chapter Five: A Better Pill to Swallow

In Chapter Five, David Sinclair traces the history of research on chemical compounds that may have longevity and vitality potential. He identifies compounds like rapamycin, metformin, resveratrol, and NAD boosters as viable options. The body's three main longevity pathways, mTOR, AMPK, and sirtuins, have evolved to protect our bodies during times of adversity. Sinclair explains that when these pathways are activated by chemical compounds like those he identified, they simulate real adversities – as such, the same benefits accrued when they are activated by real adversities can be achieved. In other words, these compounds can trigger our survival network and help us live longer, healthier lives by mimicking real adversities. He outlines the strengths and potentials of some of these chemical compounds:

Rapamycin: Initially intended for treating fungal conditions like athlete's foot, rapamycin was found to be a rather effective immune system suppressor. As a result, its prospect of potentially being used as an antifungal treatment was discarded, but it also represented potential use for other conditions. After several years of research, rapamycin emerged as an effective compound for improved vitality and longevity. Sinclair cites several research studies to support this, including one conducted on yeast, where it was discovered that feeding yeast cells with rapamycin could extend their lifespan. Normally, if you put 2,000 yeast cells into a culture, only a few will remain viable after six weeks. However, if they are fed with rapamycin, around half of them will remain viable over the same period of time. This is possible because rapamycin stimulates the production of NAD, thus allowing the cells to live longer. Similarly, fruit flies fed with rapamycin were known to live 5 percent longer, while mice fed with rapamycin also lived 9 to 15 percent longer than their normal lives. That's the rough equivalent of an additional ten years of healthy human life. However, Sinclair is quick to point out that rapamycin isn't a panacea. Rather, as an immune system suppressor, it can actually suppress the immune system over time. It's also known to be toxic to the kidney and less effective for longer-lived animals than it is for shorter-lived ones. Nonetheless, rapamycin represents progress toward using chemical compounds to achieve longevity and vitality.

Metformin: Another chemical compound with great potential identified by Sinclair is dimethyl biguanide, commonly called metformin. Widely used for treating type 2 diabetes, it is considered one of the safest, most widely used, and most effective generic medications for treating a wide range of prevalent medical conditions. Research indicates that people taking metformin, albeit for treating other health conditions were living notably healthier lives. In research conducted with mice, even a very low dose of metformin has been shown to extend their lifespan by about 6 percent. That's equivalent to five extra healthy years for humans. Apart from outright lifespan extension, metformin also impacts many diseases, offering some level of protection against cancer. Indeed, in 26 different studies of rodents treated with metformin over the years, 25 of them show proof of protection from cancer. A study of more than 41,000 metformin users between the ages of 68 and 81 concluded that the medication reduced the likelihood of dementia, cardiovascular disease, frailty, and depression – and not by a small amount. Like rapamycin, metformin mimics calorie restriction, works in a similar manner, and offers similar benefits. However, while rapamycin works by TOR inhibition, metformin activates the AMPK pathway. As a consequence of AMPK activation, more NAD is produced, which turns on sirtuins. Consequently, the entire primordial survival circuit is engaged, ostensibly slowing the loss of epigenetic information and keeping the metabolism in check, ensuring that all organs stay younger and healthier. While it's easy to assume that a medication like metformin would take a long time to show appreciable effects on aging, Sinclair explains that the effects could be rapid. He points out that effects could begin at the cellular level within a week or even 10 hours of taking a single 850mg metformin pill. However, he also adds that there's still a lot of work to be done to prove whether metformin can reverse the aging clock in the long term.

Resveratrol: After discovering the world's first true longevity genes, Sinclair and other researchers began searching for ways to ramp up their activities in mammals without having to actually insert extra copies of the genes into their bodies. This sparked research that led to the discovery of the first SIRT1-activating compound (STAC) called fisetin and a second called butein. Unfortunately, none of these STACs held enough prospects for further research. However, while exploring compounds with similar structures to butein and fisetin, another STAC, resveratrol, emerged. When Sinclair tested resveratrol on yeast, he discovered that it was much more effective for prolonging its lifespan than butein and fisetin. The compound was able to prolong the lifespan of yeast to up to the equivalent of 50 extra healthy years in humans. He also discovered that the compound was able to extend the maximum lifespan of the yeast cells. Sinclair also gave the compound to his fellow researcher, Marc Tatar, to try out on insects. Once again, the results were favorable. Fruits flies live for an average of 40 days. However, when Tatar fed fruit flies with resveratrol, they experienced an average lifespan extension of ten days. Similar studies on roundworms and even human cells likewise yielded favorable results. Studies of resveratrol have since opened the way to research into other sirtuin-activating compounds (STACs).

NAD boosters: NAD was discovered in the early twentieth century and used as an alcoholic fermentation enhancer. Owing to its ability to improve alcohol, scientists carried out more research on it, resulting in the discovery of its benefits in fighting diseases and the aging process. Research showed that just like resveratrol, NAD was a sirtuin-activating compound, perhaps even more effective. NAD serves as fuel for sirtuins, while without NAD, sirtuins can't work efficiently, and consequently cannot extend life. Unfortunately, NAD levels decrease with age throughout the body. Sinclair and his fellow researchers set out to study the effects of boosting NAD levels and safe ways to do so. They were able to identify the gene that makes NAD in yeast, called PNC1. Sinclair and his fellow researchers discovered that by introducing extra copies of PNC1 (which converts vitamin B3 to NAD), they were able to boost NAD levels in yeast and consequently extend its lifespan by as much as 50 percent. Sinclair explains that it is theoretically possible to replicate a similar process in humans. He points out that the technical know-how and technology are available, but that the stakes are too high to try it on humans for now.

Nonetheless, human studies using other methods to boost NAD levels are still ongoing.

Sinclair concludes the chapter by sharing several anecdotal examples of the effectiveness of the medications or compounds shared in the chapter. For example, he explains that his father has been using metformin and a NAD booster called nicotinamide mononucleotide or NMN, which has thus far proven effective.

Chapter Six: Big Steps Ahead

In Chapter Six, David Sinclair reemphasizes the possibility of a not-so-distant future in which the "aging disease" can be treated. He outlines a wide range of exciting new paths in medical research that hold great potential, boldly asserting: "Aging is going to be remarkably easy to tackle. Easier than cancer." He continues Chapter Six by discussing current trends and advancements made in medical research, more specifically in the field of aging. One such advancement, he describes, is the research and development of senolytics, which are a class of pharmaceuticals designed to eliminate senescent cells. To emphasize the implication and importance of senolytics, Sinclair provides an in-depth explanation of the effects senescent cells have and the potential they hold to counteract aging.

He starts by tracing the history of senescent cells and their effects on the body. According to him, we are victims of "antagonistic pleiotropy" caused by evolution. Put simply, antagonistic pleiotropy means that the survival mechanism that helps us when we are young can actually come back to bite us when we are old. In this case, Sinclair explains that the primordial survival circuit that has been passed down to us from a very long line of ancestors – which helped our species survive this long in the first place – has ironically evolved to make our cells eventually lose their identities and cease to divide. These cells that lose their identities and stop reproducing are technically supposed to be dead, but they aren't – that's why they are sometimes called zombie cells. You may recall that one of the key hallmarks of aging is the accumulation of senescent cells. These zombie cells are senescent and are part of what makes us age. In some cases, these cells sit in our tissues for decades, secreting cytokines that cause inflammation and attract immune cells called macrophages which then attack the tissue. This inflammation caused by cytokines has been established as a major driver of age-related health conditions. Even a small number of zombie cells can wreak havoc because the cytokines they secrete can – just like in zombie movies – cause nearby healthy cells to become zombies as well. As this keeps happening, over time, it results in some form of a biological zombie apocalypse. This apocalypse can manifest as tumors, cancer, heart disease, dementia, or other age-related diseases caused by cytokine-triggered inflammation.

Since the accumulation of senescent cells causes aging, Sinclair explains that the best thing to do is kill them off. This is exactly what the class of pharmaceuticals called senolytics, currently in development, are designed to do. If successful, Sinclair explains that the implications would be enormous. A one-week course of a working senolytics would be able to offer immense rejuvenation benefits and an age-reversal boost. Sinclair explains how senolytics would impact our health and the enormous potential it holds for mankind.

However, senolytics aren't the only exciting prospect on the table. Sinclair also discusses the possibility of an anti-aging vaccine. This, he explains, would work by priming the immune system to attack and eradicate senescent cells. According to him, some scientists, including Judith Campisi from the Buck Institute for Research on Aging and Manuel Serrano from Barcelona University, are already working on the idea. These two scientists believe that senescent cells, like cancers, remain invisible to the immune system by waving little protein signs that say, "No zombie cells here." As a result, these cells trick the immune system into letting them hang around to wreak havoc. If Campisi and Serrano are right, removing these little fake signs would make our immune system see those senescent cells and eliminate them. According to Sinclair, just as we currently have vaccines to protect babies against polio, measles, mumps, and rubella, in a few decades, we may also have vaccines that will prevent senescence when we reach middle age.

Sinclair also discusses another prospect in aging research: the Yamanaka factors. Yamanaka factors are sets of four genes – Oct4, Klf4, Sox2, and c-Myc – that can induce adult cells to become pluripotent stem cells, which are immature cells that can be coaxed into becoming any other cell type. Put simply, scientists could induce cellular age reversal; a way to make old cells young again. According to the information theory of aging, we become old and susceptible to disease because our cells lose youthful information. However, cloning, where cells from old animals are used to make healthy young animals, has shown that the information loss that occurs in cells isn't irreversible. This means that old DNA retains the information needed to become young again. Even when information is lost or epigenetic noise comes into play, there's some form of biological backup that holds an original copy of the cell's information, which we can revert to – though scientists are yet to find this backup. This is why Sinclair believes that by exploring the Yamanaka factors, we can reverse aging. He explains how a possible Yamanaka treatment would work:

An individual would get a week's course of three injections that introduce an engineered virus, which would cause a mild immune response – less than that commonly caused by a flu shot. This engineered virus, the adeno-associated virus (AAV), which has been known to scientists since the 1960s, would have been modified so that it doesn't spread or cause illness. This version of the virus would carry some Yamanaka factors and perhaps a fail-safe switch that could be turned on with a well-tolerated molecule such as doxycycline. Initially, nothing would really change in the way the individual's genes work. However, when the individual begins to see or feel the effects of aging, maybe around his or her mid-40s, he or she would be prescribed a month's course of doxycycline. With that, the Yamanaka factors would be activated and immediately start the rejuvenation process. Gray hair would start to disappear. Wounds would begin healing faster. Wrinkles would start fading. Organs would regenerate. The individual would think faster, hear higher-pitched sounds, and no longer need glasses to read. Their entire body would feel young again. He or she would start feeling like they are 35, then 30, then 25.

This isn't all hypothetical. Sinclair explains that a similar process has been carried out successfully in mice, with those treated with the Yamanaka factors living 40 percent longer than their untreated siblings. Sinclair explains that success in this frontier of the fight against aging isn't very far away anymore. Research is already in advanced stages, and more is being done every passing day to make it a reality.

Chapter Seven: The Age of Innovation

In Chapter Seven, David Sinclair discusses pervasive flaws in diagnosis processes and the medical system as a whole, while also sharing innovations in medicine that will plug these gaps. Among some of the innovations, he highlights the precision of DNA sequencing technology. He explains the impact of this technology by narrating the story of Kuhn Lawan, an elderly Thai woman who was wrongly diagnosed with lung cancer. The doctors who made the diagnosis weren't necessarily wrong – at least in the context of prevailing medical thinking. They had simply done what doctors all over the world do: follow an empirical process of diagnosis and intervention that leads to positive outcomes in "most people, most of the time." Unfortunately, as Sinclair explains, "most people, most of the time," isn't enough coverage for everyone. This means there was a chance that Lawan was getting the wrong care even though the care her doctors provided was considered correct. When doctors find cancer at the location they found in Lawan's body, in the majority of the cases, it's lung cancer, so when Lawan's doctors found her cancer in that location, they diagnosed lung cancer and tailored the care they provided to treat this condition. However, it wasn't lung cancer – instead, doctors later discovered that Lawan had a solid form of leukemia growing in her lungs. This discovery was only possible thanks to a precision DNA sequencing of her lung tumor biopsy. Rather than predicting the type of cancer a patient has by using the location in which cancer is found, Sinclair explains that precision DNA sequencing can offer a better and more precise individual-based diagnosis. It can also offer an immense amount of information about a specific patient's cancer – information that can help tailor treatment for greater effectiveness.

Just as a generalized cancer diagnosis approach didn't work for Lawan, Sinclair advocates for a shift from prescribing medicine as though we all respond to them in the same way. He points out that our sex or even our genomes can make a huge difference. This is why, he explains, we must embrace more personalized healthcare delivery more than ever. Already, such approaches are showing results, and Sinclair explains that we are gradually shifting toward more of this. Quoting Julie Johnson, the director of the University of Florida's Personalized Medicine Program, Sinclair explains: "We are about to enter a world in which our genomes will be sequenced, stored, and already red-lighted for treatments that have been demonstrated to have adverse effects on people with similar gene types and combinations as we have." He goes on to discuss several biotechnological innovations that will help doctors and the entire health care system deliver more patient-specific care to people. He expresses hope for radical advancement in the field of medicine and explains that we are on the way to a fundamental shift in the way we search for, diagnose, and treat disease. He points out that soon, our often flawed, symptom-first approach to medicine is going to be eroded, giving way for innovative and better ways of doing things. According to Sinclair, DNA monitoring technology will alert doctors to diseases long before they become acute. Our medical system will be able to identify and begin to fight cancer much earlier, before it poses a substantial threat. A breath analyzer will detect an immune response beginning to develop before things get out of hand. He outlines several biotechnological innovations that are already either being considered, currently under research, or in development.

Part 3: Where We Are Going (The Future)

Chapter Eight: The Shape of Things to Come

In Chapter Eight, David Sinclair discusses the social, political, and economic implications of longer human lives. He outlines several problems that may likely arise as we push our lifespan much further along, and discusses the implication of longer lives on the social security system of countries like the United States and those in Europe. In the United States, for instance, he explains that the social security system is already experiencing serious strain. With added large amounts of elderly patients, the system may be pushed to the precipice without targeted government intervention. He explains that the ratio of workers to beneficiaries in the social security system is currently an unsustainable three to one. Put simply, it means that for every three young people who work and pay into the social security system, there's one beneficiary. While this may not sound entirely concerning, that ratio was forty-one to one a few decades ago. For every beneficiary in the social security system, they were around forty-one workers funding their paycheck. However, as times improved, life expectancy improved and more elderly patients came into the system – the ratio thus dropped significantly. Sinclair expresses concern about a disaster that could potentially occur within the social security system if more people lived longer lives. The ratio would inevitably reach breaking point. Sinclair explains that there's no easy answer to this. Although longevity drugs and health span therapies may very likely help elderly patients feel better and stay healthier for longer, asking them to return to work in an attempt to alleviate stress on the social security system might not be well-received. He explains that for people who spend around 45 years working physically tough jobs such as mining, it would be totally unfair to ask them to return to work. He points out that when it comes to improved lifespan, for humans to have less impact on the social security system, the government would need to make decisive preemptive decisions.

Still using the United States as an example, Sinclair explains that using drugs to prolong lives would inevitably create a much wider class divide than is currently prevalent. As early as the 1970s, members of the American upper class weren't just wealthier, but were also enjoying longer lives. Those in the top half of the economy were enjoying an average of 1.2 more years of life than those in the bottom half. Fast-forward to the 2000s and that figure has changed dramatically. According to Sinclair: "Those in the upper half of the income spectrum could expect nearly six additional years of life, and by 2018, the divide had widened, with the richest 10 percent of Americans living thirteen more years of life than the poorest 10 percent." The impact of this divide is enormous. By living longer lives, the rich are able to get even richer. Extra years offer more time to oversee business ventures and make more profitable investments. Of course, in becoming richer, they are also able to afford things that help them live a little longer. Riches provide wealthy people with access to some of the world's best doctors and nutritionists, as well as to the latest medical therapies. Sinclair expresses concern that longevity drugs will perpetuate this disparity. He explains that unless aging is considered and given the attention of a medical condition by governments, only the wealthy would be able to afford longevity medication. This would bring about a period of enormous disparity between the rich and the rest of the world. It would lead to a bolder line dividing the haves and the have-nots, unlike anything the world has experienced since the dark ages. Sinclair explains that unless we take action to ensure equality when longevity is achieved, we would be pushed to a precipice where the extremely wealthy would ensure that their children and even pets live much longer than the poor. We would be forced to live in a world where rich and poor are not separated only by a differing economic experience, but also by the very ways that define our lives as humans.

Aside from social security headaches and socioeconomic disparities, Sinclair also expresses concern about the effects of prolonged human lives on our planet's population. He discusses projections made by several scientists that our planet is shifting dangerously close to its maximum carrying capacity. In 2002, Earth's human population was around 6.2 billion. A decade and a half later, 1.2 billion were added to that number. When humans are able to live much longer lives, the Earth's population and indeed the planet's carrying capacity would be stretched toward its limits. Sinclair isn't just concerned about space – he also expresses concern about thinning resources; a near inevitably as the human population grows. We'll be using more food, more water, and more everything else, which poses a major problem.

However, in as much as Sinclair outlines a host of potential problems that the prolonged human lifespan may bring, he also expresses optimism that the human race's ingenuity would help us solve these issues. Referencing the host of problems the city of London once faced hundreds of years ago, he outlines how ingenuity has helped overcome an even greater number of them.

Chapter Nine: A Path Forward

In Chapter Nine, David Sinclair builds on the progress of earlier chapters, recognizing the inevitability of breakthroughs in prolonging human lives. From pharmaceuticals like metformin and senolytics to lifestyle changes that can bring about longevity, Sinclair believes it is only a matter of time before we enter a world in which ages we currently consider as outliers become the new normal. However, he points out that this future, which he has described throughout the greater part of the book, must be fought for. He outlines certain areas that require a paradigm shift if we are to reach this future. He begins by discussing the need for more funding for aging research, pointing out that if we must make significant progress in the field of aging research, and in a way that will have wide-reaching impacts on the general population, governments must invest more in such research. According to him, in places like the United States, where the US government is still the primary source of funding for scientific research, aging research receives less than 1 percent of the total allocations for medical research. This makes the situation particularly hard for researchers studying aging. Sinclair questions why governments aren't pushing for more funding for aging research even with an evidently aging population. According to him, if a scientist has an idea or a novel way to tackle cancer, heart disease, or Alzheimer's, they'll likely receive the necessary support in funding, but the same cannot be said for aging. The way forward, he explains, is a change in how we view aging.

He explains that our society has missed the important points. We spend a huge amount of money on treating individual diseases, some of them aging-related, but we fail to tackle aging itself, which is their very core. Sinclair emphasizes the importance of recognizing aging for what it is – a disease. He also discusses the issue of consumption. He explains that while people are more preoccupied with the world's population reaching breaking point, part of what would actually make that a problem is our consumption patterns. In his words: "Longer, healthier lives will do us little good if we consume ourselves into oblivion. The imperative is clear: whether or not we increase human longevity, our survival depends on consuming less, innovating more, and bringing balance to our relationship with the bounty of our natural world."

Sinclair therefore advocates for a more innovative approach to tackle the issue of consumption.

Background Information on *Lifespan*

*L*ifespan is a medical exposé in the field of aging research. It is a science-backed beacon of hope in a world where aging and age-related diseases are not only pervasive but embraced with a sense of inevitability. It is meticulously crafted in ways that can help readers see the world through the eyes of a scientist. Published in September 2019, the book is split into three parts and nine chapters, each following a sequence and building on the progress of the previous chapters. The first part of the book lays out what we know about our past and traces how we've evolved into the species we are as humans. The second part explores what we've learned from the past, what we've achieved from what we learned, and how we achieved it, with a common theme of longevity and vitality. The third and final part of the book lays out the shape of things to come and the benefits it will bring in the scientific quest to greatly prolong human lives. The entirety of the book represents a thought-provoking narrative on aging. It demystifies aging research and longevity science for the uninitiated and brings readers intimately close to the advancements in modern medical research. In addition to discussing pharmaceuticals that may offer longevity benefits, the book also contains some actionable lifestyle changes that we can adopt to prolong our lives and ensure prolonged vitality at no financial cost. The book is recommended for curious minds who are interested in longevity or anyone who needs scientifically proven methods to improve their lives.

Background Information on David Sinclair

D r. David Sinclair is an Australian biologist and professor of genetics at Harvard Medical School. A luminary in the field of genetics and aging research, he is a recipient of more than thirty-five awards for his research and major scientific breakthroughs. These awards include the Australian Commonwealth Prize, Thompson Prize, Helen Hay, and Whitney Postdoctoral Award. Born in 1969, Sinclair is a serial entrepreneur and has been at the helm of affairs in some respected pharmaceutical startups. Considered one of the leading innovators of his time, he has been named by Time as one of the 100 most influential people in the world and among the top fifty most influential people in healthcare. He also sits on the board of the American Federation for Aging Research. Sinclair and his work have been repeatedly featured within prominent media publications such as 60 Minutes, Today, The Wall Street Journal, The New York Times, Fortune, and Newsweek, among others. He has a Ph.D. in Molecular Genetics from the University of New South

Wales and currently lives in Boston, where he enjoys hiking and kayaking with his wife and three children.

Cover Questions

1. What are the main ideas discussed in the book Lifespan?

2. Mention the hallmarks of aging discussed in the book?

3. Mention four chemical compounds that feature prominently as a potential cure for aging in the book.

4. How does the concept of antagonistic pleiotropy impact aging?

5. What are the three major limitations to a breakthrough in aging research highlighted in the book?

6. What steps are suggested in the book that could potentially trigger a widespread paradigm shift on the concept of aging?

7. How do Sirtuins impact the aging process, and what is cell senescence?

Trivia Questions about Lifespan

1. Who is the author of the book, Lifespan?

2. What was the name of David Sinclair's first lab?

3. How many parts and chapters make up the book?

4. Do you agree with the author's view that aging will be easier to cure than cancer?

5. In which chapter did the author mention his age?

6. Which chapter of the book discusses the possible implications of prolonging human lives?

7. What is the name of the contributing author of the book?

Trivia Questions about David Sinclair

1. What Major contributions has David Sinclair made to the global research on aging?

2. What does David Sinclair do besides being a professor at Harvard?

3. What can you say inspired David Sinclair to write this book?

4. How would you describe David Sinclair's optimism towards finding a cure to aging?

Discussion Questions

1. In your opinion, what would be the most concerning consequences of using medicine to greatly prolong human lives?

2. Considering the prevailing predisposition to ethical consideration, how well do you think the world's population will embrace medications that can greatly prolong human lives?

3. Which of the hallmarks outline in the book *Lifespan* would you consider relatively easier to tackle by science?

4. Do you believe aging is a disease and can be cured? If yes, what is your most logical estimate — in years — before a definitive cure to aging can be discovered?

5. David Sinclair's *Lifespan* doesn't just promise longevity, but also prolonged vitality. Do you believe that humans can ever retain much of their vitality at a prolonged age of say 150?

6. Do you think scientists, including David Sinclair, are playing God by trying to counteract the aging

process? If yes, what ethical reservations do you have about it?

7. Without considering any religious account of creation, — like Adam and Eve — what's the possibility of David Sinclair's *Magna Superstes* narrative being true?

8. In your opinion, do you believe a cure for aging — if and whenever found — would be generally available or a reserved luxury for the elites?

9. Apart from cell senescence, what other biological phenomenon do you think supports the idea of antagonistic pleiotrophy?

10. Do you think aging should be given as much attention as cancer and other prevalent health conditions? If yes, why? If no, why?

Thank You!

If you enjoyed this summary book, it would be greatly appreciated if you left a review so others can receive the same benefits you have.

Your review will help us see what is and isn't working so we can better serve you and all other readers even more.

Before you go, would you mind leaving us a review on Amazon?

Warmly yours,

The Spark Reads Team

Made in United States
North Haven, CT
01 October 2023

42251362R00039